NORWICH
a fine city

JARROLD

Pictures Richard Tilbrook   *Research* Rachel Young
Words John Timpson   *Design* Geoff Staff

NORWICH, A FINE CITY
Designed and produced by Parke Sutton Limited, 8 Thorpe Road, Norwich NR1 1RY
for Jarrold Colour Publications, Barrack Street, Norwich NR3 1TR

Text copyright © 1988 John Timpson

Photographs copyright © 1988 R H Tilbrook and Jarrold Colour Publications

ISBN 0 7117 0357 4

The black and white prints are reproduced by kind permission of Norfolk Museums
Service (Norwich Castle Museum and Bridewell Museum), Colmans of Norwich,
Jarrold and Sons Limited, and Norwich Union.

NORWICH
a fine city

Pictures   Richard Tilbrook
Words   John Timpson

JARROLD

A Fine City, Norwich

When I arrived at Norwich's Thorpe railway station, nearly forty years ago, the first thing I noticed was the big sign across the exit. It announced firmly: 'A Fine City, Norwich'.

The second thing I noticed was the rain pouring down outside. It made that sign seem a little ironic. But over the years I have come to appreciate — weather excepted! — just how fine this city is.

It is not just its historical importance, though it was the biggest walled town in medieval England, and by the seventeenth century it was the largest provincial city in the country.

It is not just its splendid old buildings, though everyone knows its cathedral and its castle, and the Guildhall was the largest and finest medieval town hall outside London.

Nor is it just its multitude of ancient churches, and its even greater multitude of pubs — a pub for every day of the year, it used to be said, though that was an under-estimate — and a church for every Sunday.

It is not just the great industries it has nurtured, though it has been England's main producer of worsted cloth, a centre for printing and shoe-making, and not a little brewing.

Nor is it just its cultural heritage, though its Theatre Royal was one of the first purpose-built theatres in the country; it was the first provincial town to open a free public library, and the Norwich School of Artists is now famous worldwide.

And it is not just the remarkable citizens it has produced, though they range from public-spirited ones like the reformer Elizabeth Fry to talented ones like the infant prodigy William Crotch, who gave organ recitals when he was four; and ingenious ones like Charles Barnard, who invented a machine to make wire netting and helped save Australia from the rabbits.

The special quality that Norwich possesses is a combination of all these features. And if we delve a little further into each of them — its history, its buildings, its industry and its culture, and in particular its people, there are all manner of secret ingredients which add to the distinctive flavour of this fine city.

Here's a taste . . .

A Fine Gravel Terrace, Northwic. . .

The Saxons and their successors

When the Anglo-Saxons lived where Norwich is now they had a number of little settlements on gravel terraces by the River Wensum. One of them was called Northwic, and the name has stuck, more or less, ever since.

In the tenth century they were getting along quite comfortably when the Vikings turned up, led by King Sweyn of Denmark. They did their best to fend them off, casting up piles of earth to act as defences, but they found it was not good casting piles before Sweyn. He sacked Northwic and burned it to the ground.

The locals that survived dusted themselves down and started again. Sixty years later the new borough of Norwich was one of the most thriving in provincial England, with light industry, a market, its own mint, and even overseas trade, thanks to the river.

This success was not surprising. The Saxons of East Anglia were an enterprising lot, perhaps because their forebears had known all the Angles. But that was in 1065. You will remember what happened in 1066 . . .

For Norwich the good news was that the Normans reckoned it rated a castle and a cathedral, which are still there today. The bad news was that the old Saxon town was partly destroyed in the process. The Earl's Palace and many other buildings on Tombland were demolished, about a hundred houses were cleared on the site of the castle, and a number of Saxon churches disappeared. The remains of one church are under the east end of the Cathedral.

In the first twenty years of the Norman occupation, according to Domesday Book figures, the number of English burgesses in Norwich nearly halved, to less than seven hundred; some three hundred houses were destroyed or left to decay; and taxes rose more than three-fold.

A fine mess, early Norman Norwich.

But as the locals moved out or died off, the first of the 'incomers' moved in. These days they are mostly retired couples or long-distance commuters; in those days it was the French garrison, foreign traders, monks and Jews. The garrison had to live on soldiers' pay, but the traders did nicely, the monks rather better, and the Jews did very well indeed. There still survives in King Street part of the substantial riverside home of Isaac Jurnet, one of the richest Jews in twelfth-century England. When he died and his property reverted to the Crown, a special department of the Exchequer had to be created to deal with it.

Norwich expanded and prospered. The castle became the official residence of the King's representative in Norfolk, the Sheriff; the cathedral became the centre of the East Anglian diocese, with a Palace for the Bishop and a monastery for some sixty Benedictine monks. All manner of friars established themselves in the city. The Sack Friars were at the top of Elm Hill, the Dominicans settled off Colegate. The Franciscans and the August inians established themselves in King Street and the Carmelites moved into Cowgate. When the Sack Friars were sacked by the Pope the Dominicans took over their Elm Hill buildings — including what is now the coffee bar at St Andrew's Hall. They added a lot more, on rather a grander scale than a coffee bar; their private chapel is the present Blackfriars Hall, and the church where they preached to the citizens is now St Andrew's Hall.

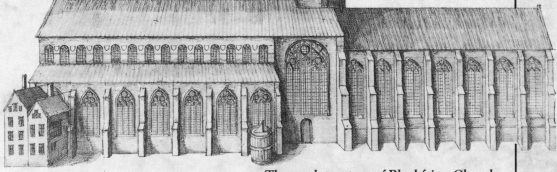

The south prospect of Blackfriars Church, once the Dominicans' private chapel.

The worsted cloth industry was booming. The merchants were able to build many fine houses. There was plenty of employment on the looms. Norwich, in short, got weaving. But with the Tudors came turmoil. Worsted exports were already declining because of competition from the Netherlands; the rich got fewer and the poor got poorer.

Fires swept through Norwich long before the Fire of London, destroying whole streets of the timbered and thatched houses. During a particularly bad fire in 1507 somebody actually took the trouble to keep count; it is recorded that 1,718 houses were burnt down in four days. Once a fire got going, not much could be done about it. The public fire service consisted of a supply of leather buckets in the churches, with hooks to pull down the burning thatch. It reached the stage where the city authorities banned the use of thatch on new buildings because of the fire hazard.

Plague took a hand as well. A couple of centuries earlier the Black Death had killed off one in three of the population. Another outbreak in 1578 did it again.

But it was not just fire and pestilence that came with the Tudors; there was persecution too. All the Friaries were closed and mostly demolished. Their possessions were seized by the Crown. The same happened to chantries, hospitals and religious guilds. And as the country went Protestant, then Catholic, then back to Protestant again, God-fearing folk found it difficult to keep up. Full marks to a pragmatic character called Osbert Parsley, a lay clerk in the cathedral during this period who kept on singing in the choir for fifty years, regardless of whether a Protestant or a Catholic was officiating. Osbert has a monument in the nave, and he deserves it . . .

While all this religious upheaval was going on, the shrewd city elders picked up a few bargains. They bought the Dominican buildings on two prime sites for £233, and the City has found them very useful ever since. They are still the most complete remains of a medieval friary anywhere in the country. They also acquired most of the hospitals, including the Great Hospital, now the longest-established old people's home in Britain, and the Carnary Chapel in the Close with its adjoining priest's house, which they turned into a municipal grammar school.

Carnary, incidentally, is not the mis-spelt origin of the Canary, the emblem of Norwich City Football Club. The word has a much less attractive meaning, simply a charnel house. The Norwich Canary was bred from the cagebirds brought over by the Dutch weavers in those same Tudor times.

With the end of the Tudors Norwich's fortunes improved again. The city had the good sense to back the winning side in the Civil War, but there were enough Royalist sympathisers to make sure there were not too many problems at the Restoration. In the 1670s it was the largest provincial town in England with a population of 21,000. Sales and exports of worsted and other textiles boomed again, and to cope with all the money that was splashing about in the city there were some of the earliest specialist banks outside London.

The most successful was founded by a Quaker family, the Gurneys, in 1775. They were linked by marriage to a London banking family called Barclay, and the connection continues in Barclays Bank, much to their mutual benefit.

Insurance came to Norwich too, thanks to Thomas Bignold, a wine merchant and banker who went into the insurance business, so the story goes, because the Sun Insurance Company refused to cover his luggage when he moved to Norfolk from Kent arguing that it was uninsurable. 'There is nothing that is uninsurable', was his majestic response. It just depended, of course, on whether one could afford the premium.

In 1792 Mr Bignold launched an insurance business in a single room in the Market Place. He only covered fire risks to start with, but the insurance idea caught on. By 1808 he was running three companies, covering fire, life and general insurance. Norwich Union was up and away.

After his death a succession of able managers continued to build up the business, and in 1887 it started its overseas operations. It has continued to expand ever since.

Since 1904, its headquarters has been the imposing building in Surrey Street, the first sight to confront the visitor arriving at the bus station across the road. It has become something of a tourist attraction in itself, with an entrance foyer so majestic that it is known as the Marble Hall.

The company is the biggest employer in Norwich, and one of the largest insurance organisations in the country. There must be many thousands of people, all over the world as well as in other parts of Britain, whose only knowledge of Norwich is through the Norwich Union.

While these new service industries flourished, traditional cloth-making declined again in the nineteenth century. It only held its own in the specialised and somewhat surprising field of shawls. Norwich shawls became the in-thing for the well-dressed Victorian lady. They were put on show at the Great Exhibition in 1851, and Princess Alexandra was given a rather superior silk one as a wedding present. Then the crinoline went out of fashion and took the shawl with it, and the industrial entrepreneurs of Norwich had to think again. The results were impressive . . .

Thomas Bignold, founder of Norwich Union.

A FORTUNE FROM WHAT WAS LEFT ON THE PLATE

The Master Mustard Maker, and other magnates

Jeremiah James Colman, great-nephew of a small-time miller, moved the business to Carrow so he could ship goods down the river, and built his first mustard mill. Colman has been the best-known name in the mustard business ever since. The Victorians used it in mustard plasters, mustard baths, mustard emetics; these days no ham sandwich is complete without it. And tradition has it, of course, that the biggest profits came from what was left on the plate.

Jeremiah James was a benevolent employer. He provided houses for his workers, three schools for their children, a canteen with food at cost price, a fire brigade with its own steam engine, and a clinic complete with ambulance and probably the first industrial nurse in the world – Philippa Flowerday, who joined the firm from the city hospital in 1878. He also installed the loudest works hooter in Norwich; when the wind was right it could be heard thirteen miles away.

Jeremiah James Colman, mustard magnate and benevolent employer.

Colmans is part of a multi-national now, but the name is still very much a part of Norwich life and the family still plays a prominent role in the city. The present Lord Lieutenant of Norfolk is a Colman.

While Jeremiah James was getting into mustard, A.J. Caley was getting into chocolates. Mr Caley was a chemist in London Street who made mineral waters on the side. In 1880 he moved to Chapelfield and launched out into cocoa, chocolates and crackers. The business, not surprisingly, went with a bang. In due course it was taken over by

An early example of a Caley's chocolate box.

CALEY'S ASSORTED CHOCOLATES
Fleur-de-Lys Works, NORWICH, England.

Rowntree Mackintosh, which in turn was taken over by the Swiss firm of Nestlé. But to the people of Norwich it will always be known as Caleys.

Shoes have been made in the city since Saxon times. They developed a turnshoe technique, first making the shoe inside out, for suppleness, and this was still being used in 1800, when there were hundreds of shoemakers in Norwich. The most successful was James Smith – his factory in the Market Place grew into the modern firm of Start-Rite. At one stage Norwich had one of the largest shoe factories in Europe. Then cheap imports hit the market, the turnshoe turned expensive, and much of what had started right ended sadly, though Start-Rite itself still marches on.

Brewing was another industry which boomed in the last century and faded in this. John Patteson produced 20,00 barrels of beer in 1801, a bigger output than many of the London brewers. By 1836 there were 26 breweries in Norwich and these were absorbed into four major ones, each with its chain of pubs. Steward & Patteson, which developed from John's early efforts, had 489. But none of those old names remain, and Norwich is reduced to one brewery – not because of lack of demand – its citizens are as thirsty as ever – but through take-overs and 'rationalisation' by the big conglomerates.

Printing fared rather better. Again there were many printers in the city in the last century, but it was John Jarrold, arriving from Woodbridge in 1823, who proved the most successful. His descendants still run the family firm, and the name remains unchanged at the London Street store, at the printing works in the old yarn mill by the river, and in its publications from Barrack Street – of which this book is a fine example . . .

The first World War provided Norwich with a new industry. Boulton & Paul made 550 fighter aircraft for the Royal Flying Corps. The city suffered badly in the second; over forty air raids, causing widespread casualties and much destruction, including more than a hundred factories and the old City station.

But in the past four decades the developers have more than made up for the losses. New buildings have sprung up as businesses have multiplied. The cathedral spire, second only to Salisbury's in height, already had to share the skyline with the red brick tower of the 1930s City Hall, unkindly described by critical citizens when it was built as 'The Marmalade Factory'. Castle Hill, dominated for so many centuries by the castle was confronted by the rather taller headquarters of Eastern Counties Newspapers. The main seat of learning is no longer the Tudor grammar school but the modern University of East Anglia on the edge of the city.

There is a lot more building still going on – some of it attractive, most of it tolerable, a fraction quite appalling. But it is the old buildings, naturally, which contribute most to the appearance of this fine city. And as with the notes in a fine piece of music, to get the best effect you need the right spaces in between . . .

John Jarrold

Watch This Space

It's been here a long time

Tombland is a confusing name for the visitor. It sounds like some sort of churchyard – particularly as it is so close to the cathedral. But Tombland in Anglo-Saxon times simply meant an open space where they held their market. It was bigger than it is now, but it was still not big enough for the Normans. They moved the market to the far larger space where it is today and Tombland, now with its trees and cobblestones and handsome old buildings, was left in comparative peace.

Even the new site of the market proved inadequate. By the Middle Ages the stalls and livestock were overflowing into the sidestreets. So there were horses in Rampant Horse Street, cattle and sheep in the Haymarket, pigs in Hog Hill (now Orford Place), wood in Timberhill, and dyestuffs in the Maddermarket – another confusing name, but madder was just a word for dye, and traders in the Maddermarket were no angrier or dottier than anywhere else. The Maddermarket Theatre, incidentally, has only had its present role as an Elizabethan-style playhouse since the 1920s; it was originally a Roman Catholic chapel.

In earlier times plays were performed in the market itself, along with processions and other public entertainments. If there was something to celebrate – a great victory, a coronation, granny's birthday – that was where it all happened. It was also where elections were held. In the Castle Museum there is still the chair, set on a platform with carrying poles, in which the successful candidate was carried around the market place and tossed up and down with great vigour – to remind him perhaps that no seat is entirely safe . . .

By the late seventeenth century the whole area was so congested that the livestock market was moved to Castle Hill. In 1960 it was moved again to the city outskirts and the old site became a car park, one of the city's less enchanting open spaces, now the site of a major new development, Castle Mall.

Down in the old market place trade continued to flourish. In Georgian times there were rows of farmers' wives sitting on the cobbles selling their farm produce out of peds, the pannier baskets which gave pedlars their name. These days there are permanent stalls and the peds are polythene bags, but the principle is much the same. The rows of different coloured canopies, which have featured on so many calendars and picture postcards, make it one of the most attractive markets in the country.

A much more placid open space in the heart of the city is the Close, the walled area alongside the cathedral, where a delightful green is surrounded by fine old buildings, and a system of axle-bending gullies across the roadway – 'sleeping policemen' in reverse – ensures that any traffic moves at a crawl, even when it has surmounted the first hurdle of getting past the custodian on the gate.

But it was not ever thus. In the Middle Ages it was a hive of ecclesiastical activity. The monks were a self-sufficient lot. They had their own granary and baked the bread in their own bakery; they ran their own piggery and swannery, and their own plummery – not a fruit orchard, a workshop for the leadworkers, later to become known as plumbers. But they did have their own orchards as well, and a dovecot to maintain the supply of pigeon-meat, and a garden of medicinal plants for the Infirmarer, and a smokehouse to preserve the Yarmouth herring. At one stage they were rebuked by the Bishop for keeping sheep on the cloister garth; nowhere in the Close, it seemed, was sacred.

They also had their own brewery, which must have been particularly popular, because after the Priory was closed in 1538 during the Reformation, the drinking continued. As late as the 1790s there were five pubs in the Close.

All this industry involved a great many people in addition to the monks themselves, from washerwomen to tailors, and many of them lived in the Close with their families. It was an independent little city within a city, over which the Norwich elders had no control. Many a fugitive dropped into the Close for sanctuary, just missing capture by his pursuers. Such a visit, I suppose, became known as a Close call . . .

Mousehold Heath, overlooking the city, was another ancient open space, much patronised by rebel peasants. They more than once made it their headquarters, and if they had stayed there instead of sallying into the city they might have survived rather longer. Mousehold was also the inspiration for George Borrow's famous reference to 'a wind on the heath, brother' – though it could apply to most heaths in Norfolk, most of the time.

George Borrow – author of the phrase, 'a fine city, Norwich'.

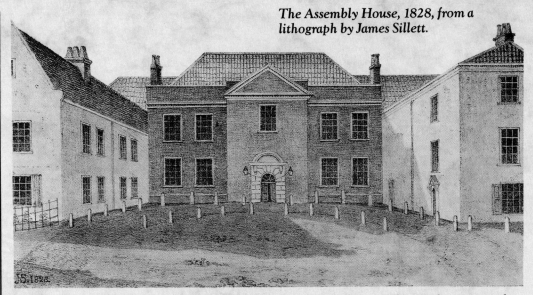

These days it still has plenty of space, offering fine views over the city. There is also an area where the view is somewhat restricted; Mousehold is the site of the present Norwich Prison.

Many medieval open spaces in the city have long since disappeared, like the Gildencroft, twelve acres of pasture between Magdalen and Oak Streets, where a notice warned the locals in Jacobean times to keep off the grass. It told them 'not to spoil the grass by immoderate Campings and Dancing'. 'Camping' in 1671 did not involve tents, or funny walks; it was a kind of mass football, as dangerous to play then as watching the modern version is today.

The Gildencroft has been built over since the 1820s, but another historic open space still survives – Chapelfield Gardens, the oldest park in the city. It was once the grounds of the College-in-the-Fields, a community of priests where the Assembly House stands now. In Elizabethan times it was used for compulsory archery practice, and by clothworkers for stretching and dying their cloth – though one hopes, for the clothworkers' sake, the two activities did not coincide.

So even an open space can have an odd little tale to tell. But some of the city's most fascinating stories are linked with its buildings – and the best known of these stories are not necessarily the best . . .

THIS PRECIOUS STONE, SET IN AN ANCIENT SEE

And not just the cathedral

Norwich Cathedral, with that marvellous soaring spire, is known throughout the world – if only because of all those insurance advertisements. Its founder was a Norman bishop, Herbert de Losinga, formerly Prior of a Benedictine monastery in France. There is no doubt that he started building it in 1096; not everybody is agreed why. The story goes that he became Bishop of Thetford by slipping the King a backhander. The figure of £1900 is sometimes quoted – a positive fortune in those days. Then he repented and went to Rome to confess all. The Pope granted him absolution and told him to carry on as Bishop, so long as he moved to Norwich and built the cathedral.

It is a romantic story, but like so much historical romance the experts now discount it. The explanation would seem to be far more mundane – Herbert happened to be a very energetic bishop. He not only built the cathedral, he created five dependent priories, founded a leper hospital to the north of the city (its chapel is now a branch library!), and built the Bishop's Palace and a monastery to go with it. No doubt he even found time to take a few services as well.

Much of the old Norman cathedral still remains, and the Bishop's Throne is the oldest in the country. That familiar spire is not, alas, the original, which fell down in a gale in 1362. It was rebuilt, only to be struck by lightning a century later. We can thank James Goldwell, who became Bishop in 1472, for putting up the present one, at 315 feet the second tallest in England – only Salisbury is higher. He also left his own distinctive mark inside the cathedral. On every boss in the presbytery there is his pictorial signature, a gold well.

In the thirteenth century, as well as the cathedral, there were fifty-six parish churches within the boundaries of the city, a remarkable number for a population of only 6,000 – though in parts of rural Norfolk today villages have dwindled so dramatically that the ratio of churches to parishioners is even higher.

Some of those in Norwich were closed down under the Tudors and three were blitzed in the last war, but Norwich still claims to have more medieval churches than any other town in Western Europe. Not all of them still function as churches. One is a night shelter for the homeless, another is a puppet theatre, a third is a centre for martial arts. St Peter Hungate has been a museum of church art and craftsmanship since 1933.

Of those that retain their original purpose, the finest must be St Peter Mancroft, rebuilt in the fifteenth century. At that time it was also probably the richest – it had three rooms packed with gold and silverware, jewels, rich textiles and illuminated manuscripts. One of its more obscure distinctions was linked with its bells; it is said that this is where ringers first developed the art of ringing the changes. They also developed quite a thirst in the process – the original ringers' jug at St Peter's holds thirty-five pints of ale.

The Church of England does not have the monopoly of fine church buildings. Norwich has been a centre for Non-conformists since the earliest group, known as the Brownists, had their headquarters in the Great Hospital in 1580. The Octagon Chapel, now Unitarian, was described by John Wesley as 'perhaps the most elegant meeting house in Europe'. He may not have intended that as a compliment; he could well have preferred the money to have been put to better use. Certainly he was not too complimentary about the local Methodists. He told them they were 'the most ignorant, self-conceited, self-willed, fickle, untractable, disorderly, disjointed society in Britain'. They seem to have survived that blast remarkably well – indeed they recently produced the current successor to Wesley as leader of the country's Methodists.

The thirty-five pint Ringers' Jug, from a pencil sketch by Henry Ninham.

The Roman Catholics used to claim, rather pointedly perhaps, that their church of St John the Baptist, just outside the city wall, was the largest Catholic church in England except for Westminster Cathedral. The point was taken; St John's is now a cathedral too . . .

The most imposing secular building in Norwich, and certainly the biggest, is the Norman castle, a massive stone cube set on a mound in the centre of the city, 70 feet high and 100 feet square. It rarely got involved in any actual fighting, and although technically it remained a royal castle until the last century, for much of its existence it was a prison. The last public execution at the main gate took place in 1867. These days there are still some gruesome sights in the castle, but only as exhibits in its museum.

Many ancient buildings in Norwich now serve this kind of role, as tourist attractions and cultural centres. The ancient Guildhall, for instance, completed in 1413 to celebrate the granting of the city's charters – not just one charter, but three – is now the tourist information office. It has been much prized over the centuries, but it may not have been too popular when it was built. A special tax was levied on the citizens to pay for it, and they had to work on it if required, for fifteen hours a day. Part of it was a prison, so they could pay for it, work on it – or finish up inside it.

The Bridewell Museum was one of many grand houses in the city built by prosperous merchants in the fourteenth century. It was 250 years before it became a Bridewell, a house of detention for beggars and vagrants. It also housed for a time Peter the Wild Boy, brought back from a German forest by George II. Having got him home it would seem the King was not too clear what to do with him, and the Bridewell was one of the places which looked after him. I recall that when the Eastern Daily Press offices were in nearby London Street I enjoyed many a beer at the Wild Man without any idea how the pub got its name. I assumed it was dedicated to one of our stranger sub-editors.

The early occupants of Strangers Hall were not strange in that sense. The term was applied to the religious refugees who poured into Norwich in the 1500s, mostly from the Netherlands. Some of them prospered greatly, and the Hall, with its vaulted undercroft and its fine Great Hall, was owned until 1700 by a succession of rich businessmen. Then it became a Judges' Lodging, and a home for Catholic priests. It was deteriorating sadly when a Norwich solicitor took it over, opened part of it as a folk-life museum – one of the first in the country – and in 1922 gave it to the city.

**Strangers Hall, now a folk-life museum.
From a sketch by Henry Ninham.**

At least two other houses with long histories are now in the culture business. Wensum Lodge, which contains part of Isaac Jurnet's original home — remember the wealthy Jew who left such a windfall for the Exchequer? — is now an adult education centre. Dragon Hall, built by a fifteenth-century merchant in King Street, has just been restored as a Heritage Centre, complete with the original red dragon decorating the beams of the splendid first-floor hall.

The Assembly House, once the town house of the Hobarts of Blickling Hall, became a rather superior leisure centre as early as 1775, where city society came to concerts and balls. Frank Noverre had a private ballroom in part of it, and might be surprised to know that his name is now borne by something as plebeian as a cinema . . .

The rest of the Assembly House had a chequered career as a Masonic Hall, a girls' school, a warehouse, a YMCA centre, and a wartime camouflage school — when its activities must have been more chequered than ever. Finally it was bought by a Norwich shoe manufacturer called Henry Sexton and given to the city for exhibitions, meetings and other cultural activities — with a licensed restaurant and bar to help the cultural conversation along.

Mr Sexton's philanthropic interest in culture was shared by other generous businessmen with a bit of cash to spare. Another shoe tycoon, Sir Henry Holmes, gave the Bridewell to the city; Leonard Bolingbroke was the solicitor who founded the Strangers Hall Museum; and Russell Colman gave the family art collection to the Castle Museum, along with galleries to put it in. But Norwich also produced people who were able to contribute something more personal to its cultural life — their talents . . .

'A FINE CITY, NORWICH' -
BUT WHO SAID IT FIRST?

Artists, writers, and assorted bestsellers

That Colman collection now in the Castle Museum is largely devoted to the nineteenth-century Norwich School of Artists, headed by two very different characters with different backgrounds, with only their artistic talent and their Christian names in common, John Crome and John Cotman.

Crome's father kept the King and Miller public house on Tombland, and he picked up his early experience as an artist while apprenticed to a coach and sign painter. Cotman's father, on the other hand, was a hairdresser and wigmaker in London Street who sent him to Norwich Grammar School, and then to study art in London. Crome acquired a wife and eleven children, and to make ends meet gave drawing lessons; Cotman again did rather better, and eventually had his own drawing school on Palace Plain. He travelled a great deal and spent his final years in London; whereas Crome never left Norwich.

But between them they launched the first and longest-lived society of artists outside London, holding annual exhibitions and selling what they could, mostly at knock-down prices. As with so many artists, their paintings only made real money after their death.

Incidentally, one of Crome's pupils was a girl called Elizabeth Gurney of Earlham Hall, now part of the University. She was wooed by a Mr Joseph Fry, who proposed to her by leaving his watch on a garden seat at Earlham. If she picked it up it would mean 'Yes'. I suppose it was the Norwich equivalent of tying a yellow ribbon round the oak tree. The plan might have misfired if the gardener had taken the watch first, but all went well and the new Mrs Fry embarked on her life of good works, ranging from improving prison conditions to providing libraries for lighthouse keepers . . .

There was no Norwich School of Writers, but there have been some Norwich bestsellers. Anna Sewell actually lived just outside the city, in Old Catton, but her book was published and printed in the city by Jarrolds in 1877, and it turned out to be a nice little earner. I have a copy of 'Black Beauty' dated 1901, which notes in the front that it was 'in its 266th Thousand'. The figures must now run into millions, and it is still selling. Its author, alas, was already ill when she wrote it and died soon after it was published.

Five centuries earlier another woman in the city was also very ill and expected to die. But as she received the last sacrament she had a series of visions and made a miraculous recovery. She too wrote a famous book, 'Revelations of Divine Love', which may not have sold millions but did make history — it was one of the first books written by a woman in English.

John Sell Cotman, one of the earliest painters of the Norwich School.

Her name, rather confusingly, was Julian, and she lived a solitary existence in a cell attached to St Julian's Church in King Street. It was a popular way of life at the time — according to the records there were fity such recluses in medieval Norwich, more than in any other town. They were fed and watered by sympathetic neighbours, the early version of meals-on-wheels. St Julian's was bombed during the last war, but it was rebuilt with a small shrine dedicated to Dame Julian.

Most Norwich people probably believe she was the nearest to a saint that the city can claim, but there was actually a St William of Norwich, a twelve-year-old boy whose body was found in Thorpe Wood on Easter Eve, 1144. The Jews were accused of his ritual murder and he was buried in the cathedral. He was never canonised, but a monk called Thomas of Monmouth looked after his shrine and wrote a book about the miracles that occurred. Few people remember either him or St William, but Thomas could well be Norwich's earliest author.

Four centuries later, Norwich produced a writer of a very different character. Robert Greene was actually a bit of a rotter. He deserted his wife and children, got heavily into debt, and devoted himself to wining and wenching as much as actually writing — a sort of sixteenth-century Angry Young Man. He eventually died, it is said, of a surfeit of Rhenish wine and pickled herring — a pretty devastating combination. He wrote various romances and plays, but he only achieved any sort of immortality when Shakespeare used the plot from one of his books for 'A Winter's Tale'. Perhaps Will pinched it out of revenge after reading Mr Greene's description of him as 'an upstart crow' — Mr Greene was not a very good drama critic either.

George Borrow somewhat restored Norwich's literary image, though he was actually born in Dereham in 1803 and only came to the city to attend the Grammar School. His school-days, as with most of us, were not the happiest days of his life; he detested the place and was horsewhipped for truancy. He spent many years travelling but returned regularly to the family home in Willow Lane and ended his days in Norwich. That famous 'wind on the heath, brother', was said to refer to Mousehold Heath. His 'Bible in Spain' was a nineteenth-century bestseller, but his picaresque style is not everybody's cup of tea. His most quoted creation was not a story or a character, but just four words, a Borrow phrase which has been borrowed again for this book: 'A fine city, Norwich'.

Elswhere in that fine city a contemporary bestseller had emerged, 'Illustrations of Political Economy'. Its author, Harriet Martineau, was born in Gurney Court, as indeed was Elizabeth Fry. She had difficulty finding a publisher — the title, after all, was not exactly a gripper — but it eventually came out in monthly parts and was snapped up by the brighter reading public. Harriet moved to London and became a leading light in fashionable society. Her autobiography provides much material for students of the Victorian social scene. For more specific reference works, however, one must turn to the real specialists . . .

ALAS, POOR SIR THOMAS
Doctors, nurses and hospitals

The statue of Sir Thomas Browne has for many years stood on Hay Hill, gazing meditatively at a Roman urn. In the seventeenth century he was a doctor, philosopher, ornithologist — he kept a bittern in his back garden — and student of urns. His most famous book was 'Religio Medici', but I rather prefer the title of 'Pseudodoxia Epidemica', or 'Vulgar Errors', which could well be borrowed for a book on modern property development.

His interest in urns led to a book about the benefits of cremation. In it appears a strange premonition. 'To be gnaw'd out of our graves, to have our skulls made drinking-bowls and our bones turned into pipes to delight and sport our enemies, are tragical abominations, escaped in burning burials.' Sir Thomas was not burned and urned, as he might have preferred, but was buried in St Peter Mancroft in 1682. And he did not escape his tragical abomination. Some 160 years later his skull was accidentally 'gnaw'd' out of his coffin by workmen digging another grave.

A local antiquary heard about it and carried the skull away, no doubt murmuring, 'Alas, poor Thomas'. For years it disappeared, until a doctor at the Norfolk and Norwich Hospital produced it from somewhere and gave it to the hospital museum. There it sat, glaring reproachfully, for nearly eighty years. Finally in 1922 it was returned to its tomb and reunited with its body.

Another Norwich doctor, Sir James Smith, was more interested in ferns than urns. He laid out a thousand guineas on the collections and notes of the Swedish naturalist Linnaeus and in 1788 founded the Linnaean Society of London, which still leads the field after two hundred years.

While Smith was pondering over plants and Browne was yearning for urns, most of Norwich's medical men were sticking to the scalpel. Thanks to them, and some inspired innovators, the city scored a number of firsts in medical history.

Their earliest achievement was the Great Hospital, founded by a far-sighted bishop in 1249 as a hospital and home for old priests; it has been a home for the elderly ever since. There were over thirty beds, with an unusual luxury in the thirteenth century — sheets. And there were four women nurses — though, presumably for propriety's sake, they had to be at least fifty years old.

The city took it over after the Reformation and local philanthropists helped to keep it going. Robert Partridge, for instance, left money so that on Michaelmas Day each resident had a quarter of a roast goose, a penny loaf and some plum pudding. There was also a daily allowance of two pints of home-brewed beer. But the old folk were not handed everything on a plate, or in a tankard. New arrivals were instructed to bring their own shroud . . .

In 1713 Norwich had the first mental hospital in the country where patients were treated instead of just being restrained. Bethel Hospital was founded by a parson's widow called Mary Chapman 'for the benefit of distrest lunaticks', as she put it in the straightforward phraseology of the day. Part of the original building still stands behind the present hospital in Bethel Street. In the summer of 1988, on the hospital's 275th anniversary, a plan was submitted to the city council for a statue of Mrs Chapman to be erected in Chapelfield Gardens. One councillor protested that the expression on the statue was 'pretty grim'. Another councillor pointed out, however, that judging by her portraits she was a pretty grim-looking lady. The plan was approved.

Some sixty years after she founded Bethel Hospital, Norwich had one of the earliest general hospitals outside London, a charitable institution maintained

Seventeenth-century author and philosopher Sir Thomas Browne.

by subscriptions. The Norfolk and Norwich was a little different in those days. There was only one resident doctor, nurses were illiterate and untrained, and surgeons operated in their old clothes so that a little blood would not matter, while the patients were drugged with rum and opium. Their speciality was removing stones from bladders; the record for an operation was 1½ minutes. The patient miraculously survived, and woke up without the stone but with an almighty hangover.

The city still had another pioneering hospital to come. In 1849 the Swedish Nightingale, the famous soprano Jenny Lind, was invited by Bishop Edward Stanley to sing in Norwich for charity, and she gave two concerts. She stayed at the Bishop's Palace, which caused tongues to wag; even in those days people enjoyed stories about bishops and actresses, though Miss Lind was a most respectable lady. The tongues were stilled, however, when the money was used to establish a children's hospital in Pottergate. At that time – 1853 – there were only two other such hospitals in the country, Liverpool and Great Ormond Street. Good old Jeremiah James Colman gave land for a new building in Unthank Road, and in recent years the Jenny Lind has become two wards in a new tower block at the Norfolk and Norwich.

Apart from hospitals, there is another kind of establishment which Norwich has been particularly rich in, which has also had a great influence on the health of its citizens – some would say for good, others perhaps quite the contrary . . .

FROM GOOD HEALTH TO 'GOOD HEALTH !'

And in the forefront: Adam and Eve

It used to be claimed before the last war that Norwich could boast a pub for every day of the year. But that was modest compared with the 1870s, when there were more than twice that number. We have the precise figure, 780, and it comes from a reliable if unlikely source, the Norwich Gospel Temperance Union. They drew up a 'Drink Map' on which each tavern was marked by a red spot. The city centre was just a scarlet blur.

I learned this through another remarkable doctor, one John Riddington Young, who came to Norwich in the 'seventies to complete his surgical studies, but seemed to spend just as much time studying pubs. He compiled details of several hundred, past and present, and visited over a hundred of them personally – and he was only in Norwich for a year . . .

His list gives a picture of the scale of drinking in Norwich through the centuries: ten Red Lions, nine White Horses, eight King's Arms, seven Royal Oaks, six White Lions, five Cocks, four Duke of Wellingtons, three Half Moons, two Rampant Horses. All they lacked was a Partridge in a Pear Tree.

Less than 200 still remain, but one or two new names have been added since Dr Riddington's day. The Louis Marchesi in Tombland is a reminder that Norwich was the home of the Round Table movement. 'Mark', as he was always known, formed the first Table for young business and professional men in 1927. He lived to see it become a worldwide organisation. Some time after his death the little Norwich restaurateur joined that other Norfolkman Lord Nelson on the inn signs of the city.

Robert Kett and fellow rebels under the Oak of Reformation. From an eighteenth century oil painting by Samuel Wale.

This recent addition is just across the road from perhaps the oldest hostelry in Norwich, the Maid's Head, one of the few places where Queen Elizabeth did not sleep, though there is a bedroom named after her. She actually slept over the way in the Bishop's Palace. But the hotel also claims visits from the Black Prince, Cardinal Wolsey and Queen Katherine; and certainly it was here that the King's commanders had breakfast before putting down Kett's Rebellion.

The oldest pub (rather than hotel) must be the Adam and Eve in Bishopgate, originally owned by the priests of the Great Hospital. It is said to receive ghostly visitations from the monks' cemetery nearby, no doubt yearning for a glass of the ale they used to brew in great quantities. It is also haunted, so they say, by the ghost of Lord Sheffield, who died in the fighting with Kett's rebels.

Thus both these old taverns have a Kett connection, and there are many reminders in the city, not only of Robert Kett, but of other Norfolkmen over the years who tried to change the course of history in Norwich; they liked to 'du different' . . .

HERE WE GO, HERE WE GO, HERE WE GO – FORSOOTH

Revolting peasants, and others

William the Conqueror had hardly got his breath back after the Battle of Hastings before his followers started plotting against him — in Norwich. Ralph Guarder was appointed Earl of Norfolk and Suffolk, and Constable of Norwich Castle — not a bad little number, one might think, but East Anglia was not enough for our Ralph, he wanted the lot. But his plot was betrayed and he fled to Brittany, leaving his wife Emma to hold the baby — and Norwich Castle. It was only a modest wooden affair in those days, but she held it against the King's troops for three months. William was so impressed by the first of the Norwich rebels — and a gel at that — he let her join her husband in Brittany.

The next revolt involved the cathedral and priory, which really saw more fighting in medieval times than the castle. The monks were never popular with the locals and in 1272 — perhaps after a glass or two at the Maid's Head — they attacked the priory precincts, destroying the main gate and the church of St Ethelbert just inside. They also damaged the cathedral cloisters and some of the monastic buildings, and generally rampaged about. The Pope took a poor view of all this, as did the King, and the citizens had to rebuild the Ethelbert Gate and its chapel. The other entrance to the Close from Tombland, incidentally, the Erpingham Gate, was erected for a more seemly reason by Sir Thomas Erpingham, leader of the English archers at Agincourt, who wanted to make a gesture of thanksgiving.

In 1381 there was a much more impressive revolt, caused by the poll tax, which raised even stronger feelings then than the new version does today. The rebels assembled on Mousehold Heath, then occupied the city and thumped several of the local gentry. The rebellion lasted for six days, until Bishop Henry Despenser, a former professional soldier, gathered some troops and sorted them out. The gentry, much relieved, are said to have presented him with the altar piece in St Luke's Chapel in the cathedral.

The next time the natives got restless, in 1442, they had another go at the priory. Again they did a bit of damage, and again it did them no good at all. This time the city lost all its privileges for nine months.

For over a century they quietened down, waiting for the big one. It came in 1549, over the enclosure of common land. Again the rebels assembled on Mousehold Heath, but this time there were 16,000 of them, with a leader who had some idea what he was doing, Robert Kett of Wymondham. They also had a more sympathetic Bishop, Matthew Parker, who came as a peacemaker to preach to them. The sermon was not an enormous success. The congregation became restive, and one of them observed loudly: 'How long shall we suffer this hireling doctor, who being waged by gentlemen is come hither with his tongue?'

Not used to such heckling, it is said the Bishop launched his audience into the Te Deum and made a hasty departure. He was better received elsewhere, and eventually became Archbishop of Canterbury. There is an annual sermon in his memory in Norwich Cathedral, but without the barracking.

Meanwhile Kett and his men, perhaps anxious to avoid any more long sermons, decided to get on with the rebellion. They swam across the river to Great Hospital Meadow, thus saving the effort of climbing the city wall, and occupied Norwich. They drove off the first counter-attacks, but three weeks later a stronger force arrived. After days of bitter street fighting they were forced out of the city and crushed. Kett was hanged at Norwich Castle.

With many rebels killed, houses burnt, Bishop's Bridge damaged and Whitefriars Bridge destroyed, Norwich had had enough, of 'du-ing different' for a while. There was never another uprising on the same scale; but there was still the odd riot to come.

The Erpingham Gate, from an etching by John Sell Cotman.

In 1570 John Throgmorton made an abortive attempt to drive out the Strangers, the thousands of refugees from the Netherlands who were doing rather well in the city. His fellow citizens, however, declined to be roused – Norfolkmen's antipathy to 'incomers' rarely runs to actual violence – and the name of Throgmorton never achieved the same fame as Kett, even as a failure.

However, in 1643 the rebellious spirits in Norwich returned to a much more popular target, the cathedral. This time it was full-blooded religious fanaticism. A Puritan mob set about sacking and looting on a grand scale, destroying carvings and monuments, smashing stained glass windows, and partly demolishing the Bishop's Palace. The Bishop had to retire to a house in Heigham, later the Dolphin Inn. The Aldermen of Yarmouth tried to get on the bandwagon and asked for the lead roof from 'that vast and altogether useless cathedral of Norwich' – but the citizens were not that daft.

The Palace, incidentally, was virtually rebuilt in the last century and is now part of Norwich School. The present bishop lives in a modern house in the grounds of the old one.

Five years after the Puritan pillaging, Norwich decided to du different again. There was another riot, but this time it was the Royalists. They attacked the homes of Puritan aldermen, and did a spot of sacking and looting themselves. When the cavalry arrived from Dereham to restore order they were attacked with pitchforks, spits, and anything else that came to hand. The women joined in too; one trooper complained that a woman 'came running out with a speete and ran the same into the ribbes of his horse, her husband then being fighting him with a holbarde.' He was obviously much aggrieved by such unfair feminine tactics.

In the middle of all this the arsenal blew up, where Bethel Hospital now stands, causing immense damage and many deaths, and effectively ending the proceedings. There were arrests and trials, and eight rioters were hanged on Castle Hill.

The next time anyone considered du-ing different from the government, over a century later, they were more discreet about it. There were many radicals in Georgian Norwich who approved of the French Revolution and thought it might be a good idea to make England a republic too. But they limited their activities to meeting in cellars and reading excerpts from Tom Paine's 'Rights of Man', which made them feel terribly revolutionary without actually going out and killing people. Norwich was nicknamed 'the City of Sedition', but that was as far as it went.

However, unemployment and high food prices did cause some rioting and in the 1840s the Chartists took a hand. They invaded church services, interrupted meetings and held secret arms drills. But for once there was less violence in Norwich than in similar outbreaks elsewhere. It was indicative of a more peaceful era to come.

That, then, is the Norwich that has been handed down to us. A city of great character as well as great historical importance, of imposing buildings and quaint little corners, rich in tales from the past but developing to face the future, a business and industrial centre as well as the heart of an agricultural county.

I had no inkling of all this on that day when I first arrived at Norwich and saw the sign over the station exit. One rarely gets the best impression of any great city from a train, and the final run into Norwich past factories and goods yards is not the most memorably aesthetic experience.

And these days, motorists do not fare much better. They have to pass through long stretches of suburban development before they reach the city proper.

But recently I have seen Norwich from the air, as I flew into the airport, and this puts it in its true perspective. There can be no more pleasing way to approach it.

For miles around there is the open Norfolk countryside, dotted with little villages and the occasional market town, but mostly rolling fields of beet and barley, bounded by narrow winding lanes. There are just a few major roads, and they all converge, as they have for centuries, on one single central hub.

The river leads there too; not the commercial waterway that it used to be, when cargo and passenger boats sailed regularly to London and Newcastle and the Netherlands, but still busy with pleasure craft.

Whether you approach it by air, rail or road, you can see it all for what it is – a fine city.

I hope you have enjoyed its story. I know you will enjoy the photographs. And may you enjoy Norwich all the more.

THE PHOTOGRAPHS

I have been privileged to live in and around this marvellous city of Norwich for most of my life, but the idea of photographing it came to me only towards the end of my professional photographic career. Since that moment I have spent over two years walking its streets with my camera, and although I am no architect or historian, I am a photographer and it is with a photographer's eye that I see the world around me.

Very soon I found myself on a seemingly endless voyage of discovery. On busy Saturday afternoons I merged with the shoppers and window gazers, when it seemed as if the whole of Norfolk was compressed into those narrow, medieval streets, whereas on Sundays I discovered a city at peace with itself, the beautiful streets quite bare of people or cars.

During that time this city and its people have come to fascinate me and I can honestly say that I never venture into Norwich without a deep sense of wonder at this extraordinary legacy from the past. This city, which most of us take for granted, is truly one of the architectural gems of Europe. Therefore I suppose you could say my pictures are the result of a love affair — a love affair with a city.

I have tried to show Norwich as a workaday city in its everyday clothing but at times a touch of magic has crept in and the familiar has been transformed. I hope that a little of the love and pleasure of taking these photographs will be shared by those seeing them.

Richard Tilbrook

The tranquillity of 'Riverside Walk' on the banks
of the River Wensum.

Bishop's Bridge *(left)*. Dating from around 1340, it is the oldest remaining bridge in Norwich. The River Wensum *(below)*, with the City Hall on the skyline.

The fifteenth-century water-gate at Pull's Ferry *(right and far right)*. Stone for the construction of the Cathedral was brought here by boat and conveyed to the site by way of a canal, now filled in.

The River Wensum from Duke's Palace Bridge *(below right)*.

The early nineteenth-century yarn mill which is now part of the Jarrold Printing works, and *(below)* the new Law Courts.

The river, seen here at Pull's Ferry *(right)*, has always played a vital part in the history of the city, and *(below right)* Friars Quay.

Vessels old and new seen from Riverside Road.

(Right) The splendour of the Bishop's Bridge at night.

Both residents and visitors find their way to
Gentleman's Walk on a Saturday morning.

Fine houses of various periods surround the Anglo-Saxon market-place of Tombland *(left and far right)*; resident pavement artists in London Street *(below)*.

Time for reflection on Guildhall Hill *(right)*.

All-important announcements are still the preserve of the Town Crier *(below, right)*.

Refreshments are available in London Street, as crowds move towards the Market Place on a busy Saturday morning.

A popular parking spot in Tombland *(below)*.

Two medieval streets now pedestrianised – Swan Lane *(far right, top)*, and Bridewell Alley with St Andrews Church tower *(right, top)*.

London Street *(below, right)*, and St Andrews Hill *(below, far right)*.

The Nut Barrow, London Street (*left*), and Tombland Alley with Augustine Steward's house (*below*). Resting in Anglia Square (*far right, top*); punks in Pottergate (*far right, bottom*); and pausing in St Faiths Lane (*right*).

The Black Tower and Walk under the Walls in
Winter. This part of the City Wall was built
about 1334.

The noble remains of the tower at Silver Road *(left)*, and the Cow Tower *(below)*, which dates from 1399.

Once captured by Prince Louis of France, Norwich Castle served as a prison for more than six and a half centuries *(right)*.

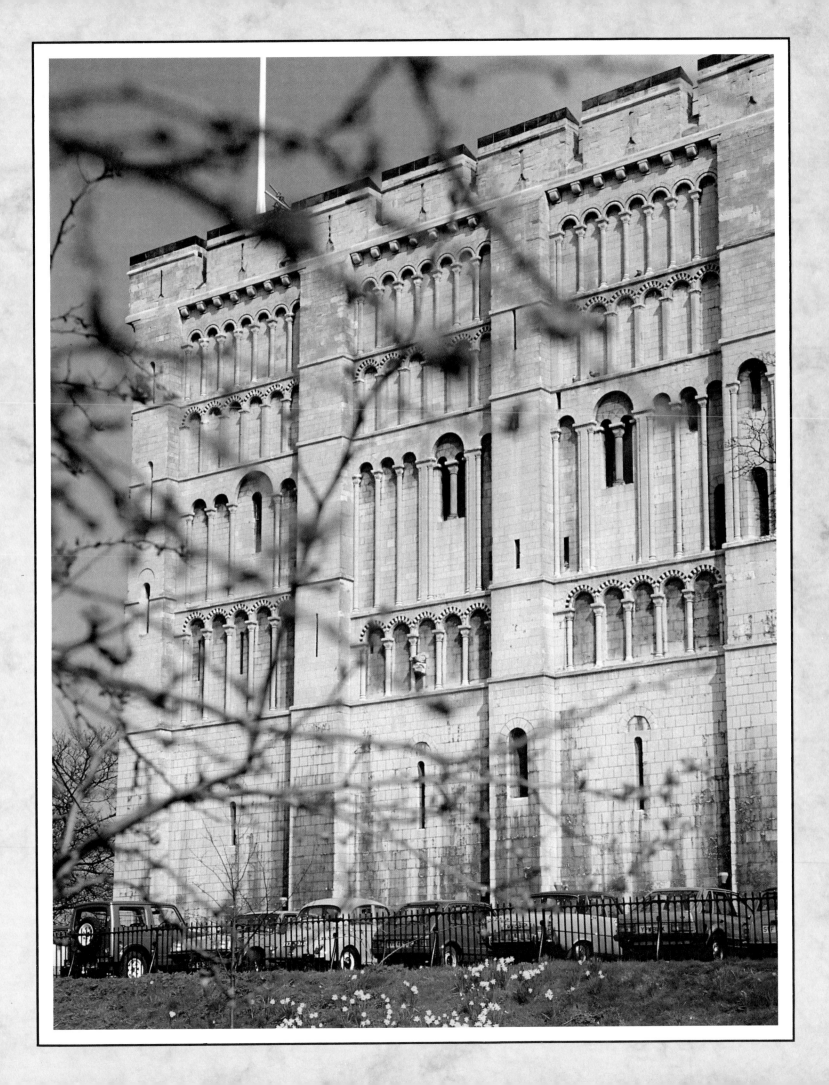

Two views of the Black Tower (*left and below*), the Cow Tower (*lower left*), and remains of the City Wall at Queens Road (*right*).

THIS FORMS PART OF THE OLD CITY WALL Built during the 13th–14th Centuries

The City Hall and Guildhall, with the Market Place. The Guildhall, completed in 1413, was the town hall until the City Hall opened in 1938.

Whether you want fruit, cheese, books, buttons or children's clothes, you can find them all in the Market.

Walking in the sun *(left)* and a bird's eye view.

Fruit and flowers.

'Season of mists and mellow fruitfulness', the Cathedral as seen from Mousehold.

(*Above, and below*) The spire at sunset.

An unusual view *(left)* of the Cathedral spire and Pull's Ferry.

The Cathedral Cloisters.

The exquisite vaulting above the Norman Nave *(right)*, and the South Aisle *(below)*.

Cathedral stalls with carved Misericords *(left)*. The craftsmen often put the faces of themselves or their enemies into their carvings.

A stone effigy *(left)*, thought to be from his tomb, of Herbert de Losinga, the founder of Norwich Cathedral, who died in 1119. *(Below)* A panel from a painted altar piece, from about 1381, now in St Luke's Chapel.

(Top, right) Canons' houses in the Close, formerly the monastic granary. *(Below)* The fourteenth-century Carnary Chapel, with bone-house below. After the Reformation, it was acquired by the city to house the Grammar school.

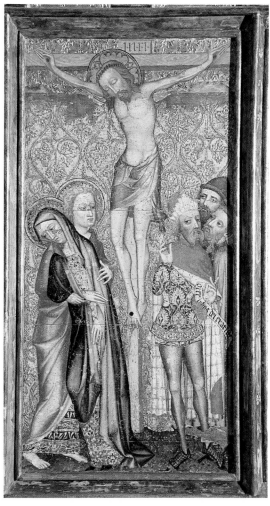

Once the old Barracks, Mousehold, now the HM Prison, Norwich — seen from an unusual angle, it looks more like a stately home.

Architectural treasures. The Guildhall (*left*), Jarrolds store facade by Norwich architect George Skipper (*above*), and a balcony on Guildhall Hill (*below*).

The magnificent marble hall of the Norwich Union offices (*far right*); a doorway in the Maddermarket Theatre (*top right*); the Erpingham Gate (*centre*); and an unusual aspect of the Norfolk and Norwich Hospital.

Contrast of old and new Westlegate *(opposite page, top, and far left)*.

The Gildencroft *(bottom left)*, and two views of the Sainsbury Centre at the University, with the Henry Moore sculpture; the Great Hospital Cloister.

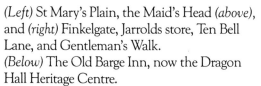

(Left) St Mary's Plain, the Maid's Head *(above)*, and *(right)* Finkelgate, Jarrolds store, Ten Bell Lane, and Gentleman's Walk.
(Below) The Old Barge Inn, now the Dragon Hall Heritage Centre.

The exterior and interior of Colman's Mustard
Shop in Bridewell Alley and the Edwardian
Arcade (*below*).

Gurney Court *(left)*, birthplace of Elizabeth Fry, the Norwich Union in Surrey Street *(below)*, and the Musick House in King Street, now Wensum Lodge adult education centre.

The Assembly House, with interior *(right)*, and *(below)* the crypt of Sack Friars, now part of St. Andrews Hall.

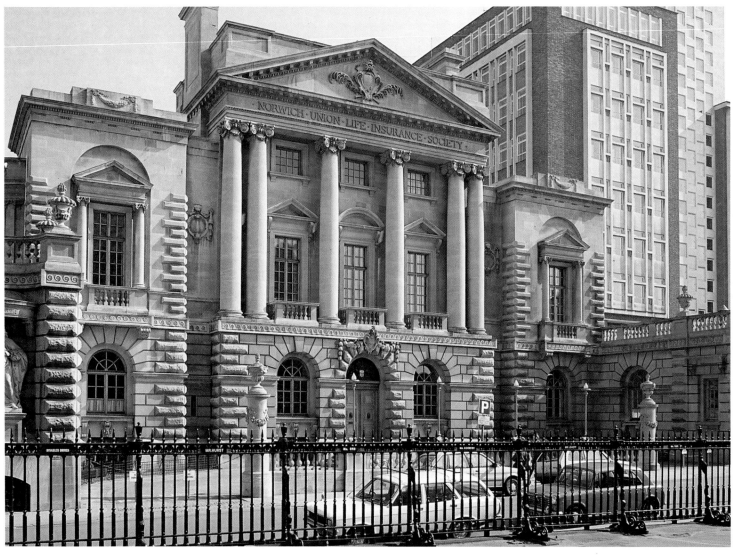

New buildings from old. The Merchant's Court was once a shoe factory, and new development on the site of an old Brewery *(below)*.

Thorpe Railway Station at night *(below)* and the interior of Barclays Bank *(right)*.

Damocles Court, Pottergate.

Doorways through the ages. Telephone House, St. Giles (1906) *(left)* and a medieval doorway to the Old Barge Inn *(below)*.

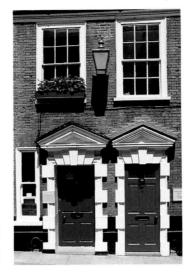

EVELYN SUFFIELD HOUSE

45

NORFOLK FEDERATION
OF
WOMEN

(Top, from left to right) Chapelfield Road, The Close, Princes Street, Mountergate; *(left)* All Saints Green and Cathedral Close *(above)*.

The Red Lion seen from Bishop's Bridge Road,
with the Cathedral in the background.

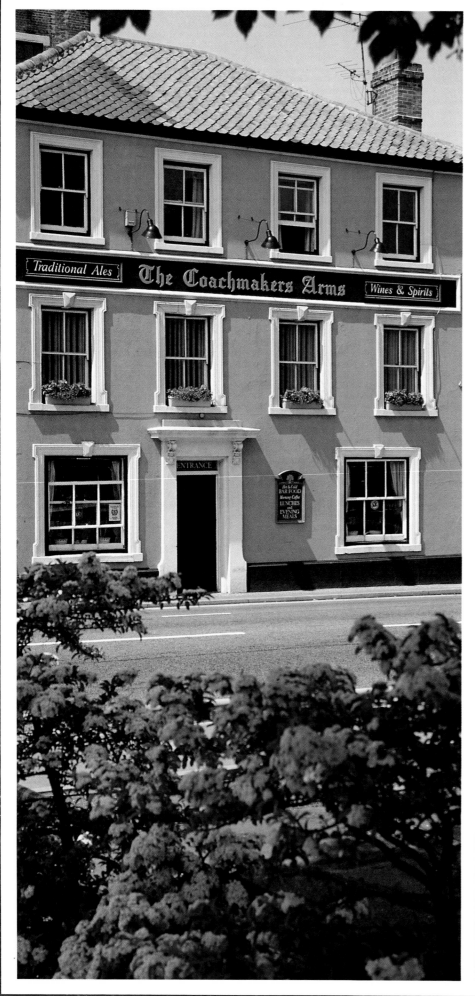

A diversity of pub names.

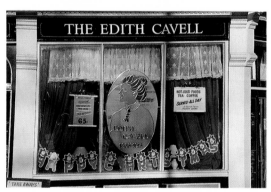

The city of Norwich was once reputed to have at least one pub for each day of the year.

In the 1840s there were over 500.

The Church of St. Peter Mancroft, rebuilt
1430-55, and the Market Place at night, seen
from Noverre House.

St. John, Maddermarket *(left)* with St. Martin at Palace *(above)* and St. Stephen *(below)*.

The clock at St. Michael at Plea *(far right, top)* and St. Benedicts Church, bombed during World War II *(far right, below)*.

St. Mary's Church, Coslany *(right)*, which has the oldest church tower in Norwich.

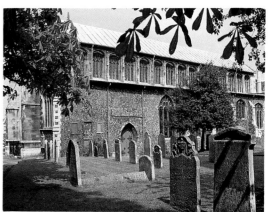

St. Giles *(far left)*, the Nave of St. Peter Mancroft *(left)* with the Font *(left)*.

St. Etheldreda *(lower right)*, St. Stephens Church *(top right)* and St. Peter Parmentergate *(below)*.

The Roman Catholic Cathedral of St. John the Baptist *(left)* completed 1910, the Octagon Chapel (1756) *(below)* and St. Peter Mancroft *(right)*.

The tranquillity of Elm Hill.

Night *(left)* and day *(above and right)* on Elm Hill.

Cobblestones, flowers, flint walls, and Georgian windows on Elm Hill.

The Britons Arms *(left)*, a fine example of a reed-thatched, timber-framed building. *(Below)* The Stamp Corner.

Chapelfield gardens, Norwich's earliest park. It
still retains its original eighteenth-century layout.

Spring in the City. The Cow Tower *(left)*, Chapelfield *(below)*, and the Great Hospital *(above)*.

Summer. Norwich seen from St. Giles
Churchyard *(right)* and Sweetbriar Road *(below)*.

Autumn. The river near Bishop's Bridge (*left*), Chapelfield (*below*) and the cemetery in Earlham Road (*above*).

Winter. The City seen from Mousehold (*above*), the Cathedral (*right*) and the University of East Anglia (*below*).

Printed in England by Jarrold Printing, Norwich.